THUNDERBIRDS™

THUNDERBIRDS: THE JOKE BOOK
© 2004 Universal Studios Licensing LLLP.
Thunderbirds © WT Venture, LLC.
Thunderbirds is a trademark of ITC Entertainment Group, Ltd.
Licensed by Universal Studios Licensing LLLP. All Rights Reserved.

First published in the USA by HarperFestival in 2004
First published in Great Britain by HarperCollins*Entertainment* 2004
HarperCollins*Entertainment* is an imprint of HarperCollins Publishers Ltd,
77-85 Fulham Palace Road, Hammersmith, London W6 8JB

0-00-718168-X

Conditions of Sale
This book is sold subject to the condition that it shall not, by way of trade
or otherwise, be lent, re-sold, hired out or otherwise circulated without the
publisher's prior written consent in any form of binding or cover other than
that in which it is published and without a similar condition including this
condition being imposed on the subsequent purchaser.

1 3 5 7 9 8 6 4 2

www.harpercollinschildrensbooks.co.uk

Printed and bound in Great Britain

THUNDERBIRDS™

BY QUINN RAYMOND

HarperCollins*Entertainment*
An Imprint of HarperCollins*Publishers*

THUNDERBIRDS ARE GO!

What do the Thunderbirds call their boxer shorts?

Thunderwear!

If the Thunderbirds ever chose a life of crime, what would they be called?

The Plunderbirds.

What did the Thunderbirds say when they rescued scientists in Antarctica?

"Thunder*brrrrrr.*"

What's the difference between thunder and the Thunderbirds?

One is a natural phenomenon, the other is naturally phenomenal.

What's the difference between the weather and the Thunderbirds?

The Thunderbirds are *always* cool!

What did the Thunderbirds have to take after they rescued people from a mudslide?

A Thundershower.

What do the Thunderbirds take when they're *really* dirty?

A Thunderbirdbath.

What do the Thunderbirds do when someone's done a good job?

Give them a Thunderclap.

What do you call a Thunderbird who's sad?

A Thunder bluebird.

What does Lady Penelope say when *FAB 1* gets stuck in traffic?

"Thunderbirds are *slow*!"

THUNDERBIRDS ARE GO!

What did Alan Tracy say when he went to the rodeo?

"Thunderbirds are *whoa*!"

If the Thunderbirds released a hip-hop album, what would it be called?

"Thunderbirds Are *Yo*!"

**What does Alan
Tracy say when his
dad makes him cut
the lawn?**

"Thunderbirds are *mow*!"

**How many Thunderbirds does it take
to screw in a light bulb?**

Two: One to screw it in, the other to turn on
the light and shout, "Thunderbirds are *glow*!"

**What's the difference between a
Thunderbird and a real bird?**

Feathers.

INTERNATIONAL RESCUE: MISSIONS ARE POSSIBLE!

What does Jeff Tracy serve with?

A tennis *rocket*.

Why can the Thunderbirds get into any nightclub?

They're part of the jet set.

**Why did
Alan Tracy
need Fermat's help breaking into the
computer?**

Because he couldn't hack it.

Where does Fermat wash his clothes?

At a laun*fermat*.

What does Parker say when he wants a day off?

"Lady Penelo*please*!"

What do you call the folds in Lady Penelope's skirts?

Penelo*pleats*.

What does Lady Penelope eat for dessert?

Penelo*sweets*.

What do you call Lady Penelope when she's in *FAB 1*?

Pretty in pink.

What does Lady Penelope say when Alan gets into trouble at school?

"F.A.Behave!"

How do fashion magazines describe Lady Penelope's style?

"F.A.B.ulous!"

What did Lady Penelope say when the Thunderbirds visited her estate?

"Don't *mansion* it!"

What was Alan Tracy called before he was made a full-fledged Thunderbird?

A Thunderbirdie.

How did Alan feel after he crashed the scooter?

Like a real Blunderbird.

What do they call Jeff Tracy?

Chairman of the Birds.

How did the headmaster know that Alan and Fermat stole the engine to his car?

They had the auto-motive.

What does Jeff Tracy say during a morning launch?

"*Breakfasten* your seatbelts."

Why was John Tracy asked to be in a music video?

He really knows how to rock-it.

Did you hear the story about Tin-Tin saving Alan from a deadly scorpion?

It was a killer *tail*.

How did Tin-Tin defeat the Hood?

She put her mind to it.

tracypower

What do you call the Tracy brothers when they have nothing to do?

The Thunderboreds.

What do you call it when Penelope is lured into trouble?

The Lady and the Trap.

What sounds stupid but is really smart?

Thunderbird-Brains.

What happens when Jeff Tracy forgets to shave?

He grows a Thunderbeard.

What happens when Alan drinks too much root beer?

A Thunderburp.

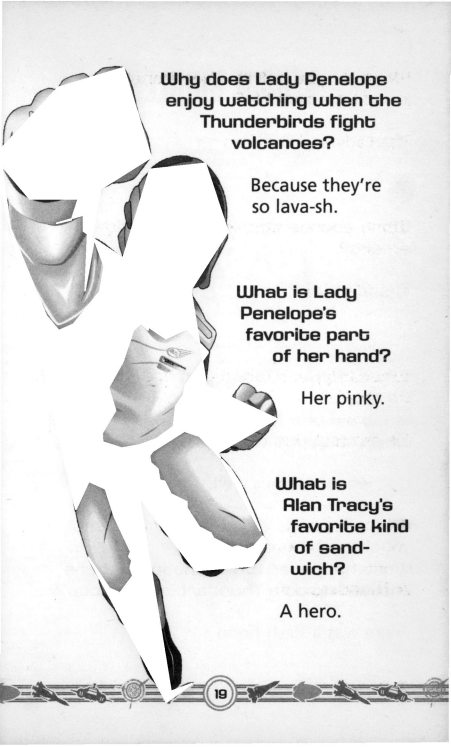

Why does Lady Penelope enjoy watching when the Thunderbirds fight volcanoes?

Because they're so lava-sh.

What is Lady Penelope's favorite part of her hand?

Her pinky.

What is Alan Tracy's favorite kind of sand- wich?

A hero.

RESCUE RIDDLES

**What did the Thunderbirds say
when they put out the oil rig fire?**

Oil's well that ends well.

**What happened when photographers
showed up to a Thunderbirds rescue?**

There was a flash flood.

What did the Thunderbirds call the earthquake that lasted only one second?

The earth-quick.

What did the miners say when the Thunderbirds offered to rescue them from a collapse?

"We can dig it!"

How did the Thunderbirds stop the stampede?

They grabbed the bull by the horns.

What did the conductor say when the Thunderbirds rescued his derailed train?

"Thanks for getting us back on track!"

What did the Thunderbirds call it when they had to fight bad guys during a hurricane?

The attack of the typhoon goons.

What do the Thunderbirds say when they stop a tidal wave?

"Wave good-bye."

ZIP, ZOOM, KABOOM!

What time is it when the Thunderbirds park *Thunderbird 1* on a fence?

Time to get a new fence.

What does Jeff Tracy say when he flies his jet to a disaster?

"*Thunderbird Two* the rescue!"

What does Jeff Tracy call his golf cart?

Thunderbird Fore!

What do the Thunderbirds call their refrigerator?

Thunderbird Ate.

What does Jeff Tracy call a vehicle when his son Alan borrows it?

Thunderbird For-teen.

What does Jeff Tracy call a vehicle when Alan and five of his friends borrow it?

Thunderbird Six-teen.

What do you call a vehicle that Alan is stuck inside of?

Thunderbird Ate-teen.

What does Parker call his tea cart?

Thunderbird For-tea.

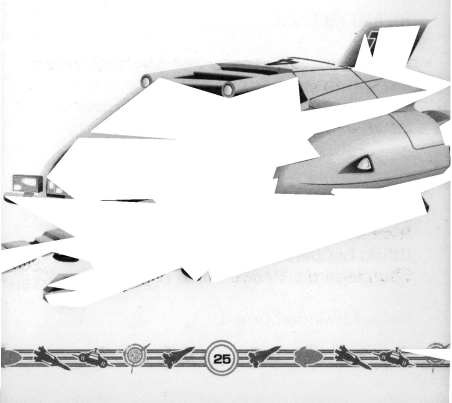

THERE GOES THE HOOD!

What was the Hood charged with when he tried to steal *Thunderbird 5*?

Rocketeering.

Why did the Hood fail?

He had no Brains.

What do you call the Hood's submarine when it comes to the surface?

An abovemarine.

What happened when the Hood stood too close to *Thunderbird 1's* jets?

He got thunderburned.

Why did the Thunderbirds have trouble capturing Transom and Mullion?

The Hood was covering them.

Why did Brains help the bad guys?

He was Hood-winked.

What did Mullion say when the Hood suggested they rob a bank?

"You read my mind."

Who's the worst person to have next door?

The neighbor Hood.

What did the Thunderbirds call the Hood when he tried to dig into the Bank of London?

A real bore.

What did the Hood say when he was accused of stealing the *Mona Lisa*?

"I was framed!"

Why is the Hood so dangerous?

He's a psychic psycho.

dangerous

Why did the Hood want to ruin Jeff Tracy?

He held a grudge after a *miner* incident.

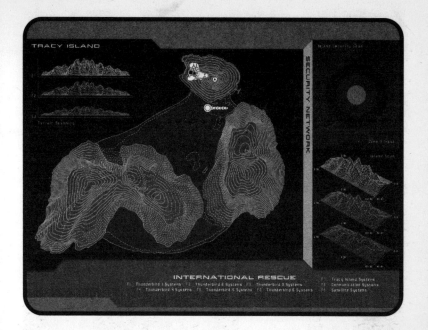

Why didn't the Hood attack Tracy Island from the air?

He would have never *planed* such a dangerous endeavor.

What is the Hood's favorite kind of sandwich?

A submarine.

Why was the Hood so tense when he was in his submarine?

He was under a lot of pressure.

Why was the Hood so hard to spot?

He was often below *see* level.

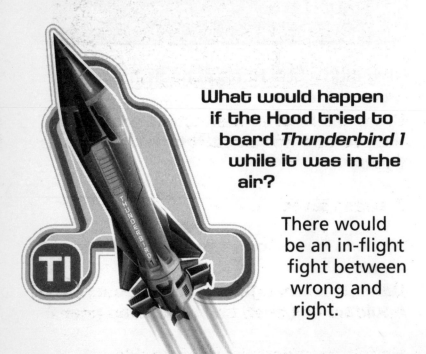

What would happen if the Hood tried to board _Thunderbird 1_ while it was in the air?

There would be an in-flight fight between wrong and right.

Why did the Hood have trouble finding Tracy Island?

He needed more *Pacific* directions.

What did Brains need when the Hood zapped the computer communications system?

A screen saver.

When Alan Tracy was at the beach, how could he tell that the Hood was near?

He felt an undercurrent of trouble.

OUT OF THIS WORLD!

Why does John Tracy like living on the space station *Thunderbird 5*?

It's out of this world!

Why did John Tracy agree to go into outer space?

He didn't understand the gravity of the situation.

Why did John Tracy miss his father's call?

He spaced out.

Why did John Tracy have a bump on his head?

He was starstruck.

Where does John Tracy go when he wants to grow strong and tall?

The Milky Way.

Where does John Tracy go to get milk for his cereal?

The *moo*-n.

What does John Tracy use to clean the area of outer space around *Thunderbird 5*?

A vacuum cleaner.

On what does John Tracy write letters?

Space *station*-ery.

How is space station *Thunderbird 5* illuminated?

With satel-*lights.*

What did John Tracy say when he first arrived at space station *Thunderbird 5*?

"This place has no atmosphere."

Why does John Tracy have trouble making friends?

He's not very down-to-earth.

How did John feel when the Hood attacked *Thunderbird 5*?

He was *star*-tled.

What does Jeff Tracy think of when he looks up at the sky?

The sun and his son.

What does John Tracy eat his meals in?

A satellite dish.

What do you call an astronaut who goes out with meteors?

A-*comet*-dating.

Wish you were here! Tracy Island

Why does John never get to have a party?

Because he can never plan-it.

What did John Tracy get the last time he tried to play golf in space?

A black hole-in-one.

**THUNDERBIRDS
ARE GO!**

How does John Tracy keep *Thunderbird 5* insect free?

He uses a Venus flytrap.

How does John Tracy defend himself on *Thunderbird 5*?

With a shooting star.

What is John Tracy's favorite snack?

Astro-*nuts*.

Why did John Tracy move off Tracy Island and into *Thunderbird 5*?

He needed space.

Why did John Tracy take a vacation?

He needed an altitude adjustment.

THUNDERBIRDS ARE GO-NE!

Knock, knock.

Who's there?

Parker.

Parker who?

Park 'er in the driveway, please.

Knock, knock.

Who's there?

Thunderbirds are *go*!

Thunderbirds are go who?

**Thunderbirds are going
away unless you open the door!**

Knock, knock.

Who's there?

Jeff.

Jeff who?

Jeff fun tonight?

Knock, knock.

Who's there?

F.A.B.

F.A.B. who?

F.A.B. the best you can be!

Knock, knock.

Who's there?

Harry.

Harry who?

Harry up, Thunderbirds, it's the end of the book!